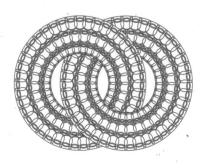

IN INHERITANCE OF DROWNING

IN INHERITANCE OF DROWNING

POEMS

DORSÍA SMITH SILVA

CAVANKERRY
PRESS

CavanKerry Press Ltd.
Fort Lee, New Jersey
www.cavankerrypress.org

Publisher's Cataloging-in-Publication
provided by Five Rainbows Cataloging Services

Names: Silva, Dorsía Smith, author.
Title: In inheritance of drowning / Dorsía Smith Silva.
Description: Fort Lee, NJ : CavanKerry Press, 2024.
Identifiers: ISBN 978-1-960327-07-9 (paperback)
Subjects: LCSH: Ecopoetry. | Caribbean poetry. | Racism--Poetry. |
   Hurricanes--Poetry. | Puerto Rico—Poetry. | Colonialism--Poetry.
   | BISAC: POETRY / American / Hispanic & Latino. | POETRY /
   American / African American & Black. | POETRY / Women Authors.
Classification: LCC PS3619.I48 I54 2024 (print) | DDC 811/.6--dc23.

Cover and interior text design by Mike Corrao
First Edition 2024, Printed in the United States of America

CavanKerry Press is dedicated to springboarding the careers of previously unpublished, early, and midcareer poets with our Emerging Voices series.

 Made possible by funds from the New Jersey State Council on the Arts, a partner agency of the National Endowment for the Arts.

NATIONAL ENDOWMENT for the ARTS
arts.gov

CavanKerry Press is grateful for the generous support it receives from the New Jersey State Council on the Arts, as well as the following funders:

The Academy of American Poets

Community of Literary Magazines and Presses

National Book Foundation

New Jersey Arts and Culture Renewal Fund

New Jersey Economic Development Authority

The Poetry Foundation

For Antonio, who inherited love

CONTENTS

BY HURRICANE

BY EVERYTHING ELSE

BY HURRICANE REVISITED

FOREWORD

In their introduction to *Aftershocks of Disaster: Puerto Rico Before and After the Storm*, Yarimar Bonilla and Marisol LeBrón make plain an awful truth: "natural disasters do more than just mar the landscape; they upend people's lives, lingering and reverberating long after the winds have died down and the waters have calmed." They and the other authors of their anthology understand all too well that man-made disasters devastate equally as much as natural ones. And that when natural and man-made disasters converge upon the same time and space, the aftershocks, the echoes, and the remnants of such disaster can imprint themselves upon the survivors of said disasters for centuries.

The convergence of natural with man-made disaster was epitomized in 2017 when Hurricane María crashed the coast of Puerto Rico at a time when the neocolonial project crashed the island's economy, resulting in the government defaulting on its loans, the PROMESA Bill being enacted, and the vampire squid of Wall Street devouring all resources. The damage María inflicted on Puerto Rico's ecology and infrastructure will take decades to recover from, but that recovery will be prolonged due to this refusal by the US to take its imperial bootheel off the throat of our beloved Borinquen.

For those outside Puerto Rico's coastal border—including we Diasporicans who have familia en la isla and visit regularly but who have a parallel yet palpably different relationship to the colonizer— the concrete and complex impact of the María/PROMESA monster on the daily lives of those who reside on the island can feel like a very real but distant abstraction, rendering their situation as susceptible to being oversimplified, overlooked, distorted, or altogether ignored. For this reason, it is essential that the island's writers provide us with testimonios that allow us a clearer path to understand what it means to live through and beyond disaster.

Dorsía Smith Silva offers us such a testimonio with her debut poetry book, *In Inheritance of Drowning*. The collection opens with "What the Poet Is Supposed to Write About a Hurricane," where, rather than focusing on the catastrophe the hurricane brings, she can't help but consider the "intoxicating possibilities and mysteries" of such an event. The poem functions as an ars poetica, a guide to how to engage with her work, as the book is instead an exploration of possibilities and mysteries that arise from the disaster's aftershocks.

In Inheritance of Drowning is also a model of poetry as protest. In her work of decolonial theory, Rocío Zambrana elucidates that for Puerto Ricans and other colonized subjects, "Protests generate discomfort by indexing the slow violence of debt, austerity, coloniality. They have the potential to dislocate by amplifying discomfort, disclosing such violence as induced." This discomfort and indexing of the slow violence of coloniality is indeed generated in poems such as "When you tap the muscle memory of the blue tarp," where the poet must decide between staying after the hurricane and being subjected to sleeping in a school shelter—where she cannot sleep because "the men looked at you like something on / the clearance rack"—or allowing a distant relative to help her relocate to New York. The "slow violence" of the circumstance reveals itself when "home turned / into, Where are you from and where are your papers?" What is being indexed here, the discomfort that is being evoked, is the impact of living in precarity. Precarity is a particular brand of "slow violence," one that is both physical and psychological. To be of the colonized, the marginalized, the othered while living through disaster and its aftershocks, is to be living in a perennial state of precarity, a precarity evident in the cycle of circular migration that most Puerto Ricans and Caribbeans are all too familiar with. The dual disasters have created a historical tendency for people to migrate to and from and to and from their place of origin in the Caribbean. Smith Silva adopts this cycle as the overarching structure of her book, which begins on the island, then takes the narrator and reader offshore to recover on the mainland, before returning again to a radically altered island.

The collection is also codified into a chiaroscuro that contrasts the sharp division between the before and after(shock) of the hurricane, exemplified by the poem "Antes/Después Huracán María." Early in the collection, the reader follows the poet as she anticipates the hurricane's arrival, as in the poem "Litany" where Smith Silva invites us into her act of preparing for the hurricane, as she gathers batteries, fills jugs with water, retrieves cash from the bank, and ties all doors with ropes and weights.

When the hurricane strikes, the poems become a documentary, capturing the moment in real time to dizzying and dislocating effect (to once again evoke Zambrana) with the poems "Hurricane," a devastated palimpsest of Wallace Stevens's "Thirteen Ways of Looking at a Blackbird," and the heartbreaking suite, "Drowning in 5 Parts." Finally, the poet carries us into the aftermath where attempts at recovery begin.

Over the course of this transition from the before to the after(shock) of the hurricane, the poet subtly and slowly shifts the focus from the natural hurricane to that man-made hurricane of the neocolonial project, where we witness the survivors struggling to move forward in the midst of the racialized, patriarchal, parasitic economic system that Naomi Klein has called "disaster capitalism" or "the shock doctrine," a system that prioritizes exploitation over rebuilding as a response to catastrophe and keeps the survivors in a prolonged state of drowning. As Smith Silva writes in "Drowning in 5 Parts," "We have always been drowning — / With sweat. / With fear. / With debt."

What Smith Silva is capturing here is the state of destierro Black and Latinx folks are forced to contend with and exist within. Yomaira C. Figueroa-Vásquez, in her book *Decolonizing Diasporas: Radical Mappings of Afro-Atlantic Literature*, qualifies destierro as "banishment, with all its accompanying and impotent anguish. Literally, it means to be uprooted, to be violently torn from the Earth." The hurricane and contemporary colonialism are major players in this mass uprooting. It leaves the uprooted to rebuild and resow and rebuild and resow all to keep from drowning again and again.

I want to bring you back to Smith Silva's opening poem, when she professes to see new possibilities in the face of the hurricane, because therein lies the power of *In Inheritance of Drowning* as a work of poetry of protest. It is not enough to document the slow violence of colonialism, the destierro, the aftershocks, the loss. In the second half of the book, Smith Silva moves beyond this in an attempt to envision something new, something else. Evident in the work of Caribbean poets such as Kamau Brathwaite, Chris Abani, Naomi Ayala, and Nancy Morejón, the reinvention of hope, the call for rebirth or renewal, is a common engine of Caribbean poetry of witness and protest. This essential element of Afro/Latinx Caribbean diasporic literature is rooted in what Figueroa-Vásquez identifies as "decolonial love." Figueroa-Vásquez explains decolonial love as "a practice that bears witness to the past while looking toward a transformative and reparative future by unraveling coloniality, the matrix of power that is manifested in our contemporary conceptions of power, gender, and bodies." *In Inheritance of Drowning*, Smith Silva reaches toward this kind of radical love during the collection's culminating sections. We see this in "Ghost Talker Poem," a poem about all the "black girls / that go missing from / newspaper headlines," but that ends with these "ghosted" girls taking "victory laps every night." We see this in the poem "Mad Love for Philly," the poet's hometown, and "Memories of Cane," which begins with plantation violence but ends with the sugar in the poet's afternoon tea sparkling as "sweet hallucinations." And we see it in "They came for us," which flips the script on the tourist/invader/colonizer, framing them as the fairy tale monster that has lost its power now that we have grown up and don't believe in their mythological power anymore. The book closes with the hurricane returning, as we know it will, over and over, but with each recurrence arrives change, mystery, possibility, and new manifestations of radical love.

Bueno, I'm done, I swear. I'll leave you to discover the wonders of *In Inheritance of Drowning* for yourself, pero please allow me to leave you with something a little less cerebral and scholarly about the poet. I had the pleasure and honor of working with Dorsía when she attended my Agents of Change workshop on writing the political poem, where I was given the privilege of experiencing her keen intellect, bright spirit, and commitment to activism and to radical empathy. Dorsía was generous with the work of her peers, and she was always excited to share and to learn from them. As the group leader and facilitator, I found myself learning just as much from her as I was teaching them. When I received the manuscript for this collection after agreeing to write this foreword, I was not at all surprised to find how rich and expansive the collection was, how in handling her subjects Dorsía extended a great deal of sensitivity and compassion—not only to those subjects who experienced Hurricane María firsthand alongside her, but to everyone impacted, including Diasporicans like myself. What you are holding is the work of a poet who sees you, who is ready to march and sing and weep and celebrate and rebuild with you, someone who desires and actively works toward a better future for us all, on the page and off. Get ready for all the gifts that *In Inheritance of Drowning* is about to offer you.

Pa'lante! Pa'lante!

Vincent Toro,
Author of *Hivestruck*

BY HURRICANE

Hurricane Irma, a Category 5 storm, struck Puerto Rico on September 6, 2017. Two weeks later, Hurricane María ravaged the Caribbean. When it reached Puerto Rico on September 20, 2017, Hurricane María was a strong Category 4 hurricane that caused massive damage to Puerto Rico's power grid, buildings, homes, and vegetation. It was later upgraded to a Category 5 hurricane.

Hurricane María killed between 4,600 and 5,800 people in Puerto Rico and caused a blackout that lasted over seven months. It is estimated that the damage was $90 billion.

Hurricane season begins in June and ends in November.

WHAT THE POET IS SUPPOSED TO WRITE ABOUT A HURRICANE

What the poet is supposed to write about a hurricane
should be skylights of horror,
not skip rocks of beauty in walls of wind,
affixed to the puzzle pieces of the vortex eye,
spinning like a lost continent's soul.
How the lively whips should stun the mouths of gravity,
hissing without hesitation,
engulfing the stench of uprooted dirt and grass.
The poet is supposed to decode the stanzas,
shudder the name María
into frail syllables:
to wish a hurricane a fast and gritty death,
not say its stubborn slow dances
held intoxicating possibilities and mysteries.

FIRST POEM BEFORE HURRICANES

·

/ˈhər-ə-kān/
a tropical cyclone with winds of 74 miles (119 kilometers) per
hour or greater that is usually accompanied by rain, thunder, and
lightning, and that sometimes moves into temperate latitudes

·

Last delicious sound,
before exiled buildings
rush into graves. Wind
is still unstirred. Innocence
herds up to chin. What the sun
remembers: our naked legs
in grass so worth parading
that eyes can't take flight. Set
the telescope to 18°23' N, 65°58' W,
before guessing which wild stump
will be mistaken for home. What building
can shoulder out of darkness.

·

NOTE: *Hurricane* has traditionally been used especially when
naming or referring to storms occurring in the western
Atlantic; it is used for storms in the northeastern Pacific as well.

·

Hurricane gnawing across alerts.
Figure A. Siren. Figure B. Siren. Siren.
No apologies to los desaparecidos.

Maybe we should notice
the rain as a cruel friend,
slightly different than what
we are used to. Each droplet
a misunderstood life.

·

huracán

huracanado

tromba

ciclón

el ojo de la tormenta

ojo del huracán

vientos huracanados

·

Hurricane races
across weaponized wind.
Ceiba trees go headless.
Flor de Maga calls herself
lucky. No, a lash to fall face
down into dirt. Palm trees
and beachside condos are hard flung
into the ocean's skirt. We dare
to say that we are thick-skinned.
That every good citizen knows
how to patch green back together,
how to shape what is meant to last.

THE AWAKENING OF HURRICANE MARÍA

At first, the rain comes in whispers:
thin slants on the windows, then it scrawls
across the glass like long graffiti,
reaching out to stretch mark the gutters
and dwarf the downspouts. The birds vanish
past the flamboyán trees: a quick foreshadowing
of the sky gaping in steep clouds. Thunder shutters
through the treetops, while lightning siphons
off the breath like fragrant heat. The rain plunges
in the arched breezeways, decapitating the hibiscus
and beehive ginger into matted limbs. The afternoon
takes me hostage: wind whipping my forlorn face,
kidnapping the right side of skin. What more do I
have to give. Not even a turn to God to rebuke the hours.

LITANY

To prepare for the hurricane,
you must gather the batteries,
especially the AA and big fat D packs.
You must wash every scrap of clothing.
You must fill every crevice and container with water,
including the rusty tub and old gallon jugs.
You must take your hard-earned cash from the bank
and hope that your money magically lasts
until the next check appears.
You must cook all of the meat
and say farewell to your milk and eggs.
Well, they were bad for your health, anyway.
You must fill up both cars with gas
and return to the station to fill three red containers.
You can never have too much gas, you know.
You must buy sheets of wood and nail them over the windows.
You must tie the doors with rope and weights.
You must bring your plants, mosaic tables, and chairs inside.
You must check your email and leave a response:
I'll be away from my correspondence, due to Hurricane María.
You must watch your favorite show and listen to the classics.
It will be a while, until you will have these sounds again.
You must gather your important papers
and protect them with plastic Ziploc baggies.
You must find your earplugs to block out
the competing noise from the neighbors' generators.
You must make friends with the neighbors.
If you are nice, maybe they will give you some food
or water later or even let you run an extension cord
to have some power from their generator.
You must say goodbye to vanity,

since you will no longer be able to blow dry
your hair or press your clothes.
You must fasten this list to memory and then pray,
until you hear it is finished.

IN SEARCH OF SPACE (AFTER HURRICANE MARÍA)

The man and I share a fixed gaze.
His bare chest is trapped in sweat
and coated with brown sunspots
like root patterns, concentric circles, misled tangents.
We are steady in the grocery line,
braving the heavy heat.
He has the certain look of a predator.
His eyes could further bend the trees,
make them snap like a science experiment.
His mouth could probably burst windows
like a scorched opera note.
And his fingers would bend metal
like a mischievous hat trick.
Yet, I could look at him forever:
become trapped in his named hunger.
We inch up a millimeter and leave
no quiet cracks between us.
Yet, we hang there in the cruelty of narrow space,
our feet holding onto our bodies
trying to pull out of nothing,
drowning around us.

THE BEE

After Hurricane María, you spin in a daze—
punch-drunk from the fetid fumes of the generator,
but you have made a decision to eat, live.

You leap onto a dark tan bra that
is wildly flapping on the clothesline,
eager to gather something sweet
and bring it to the surface.
And yet, there is nothing there but a
bare circle of cotton.

You wonder how the hurricane galloped away
with the flowers, triggering a vanishing act.
Well, where is the magician's wand
to bring back the canopy of blossoms?
It must be in the wind of loss,
along with the why and because.

There is no way to tell you
about the aftermath's slow cruelty;
it is a tale that claws cell by cell,
leaving wings to litter this earth.

DRIVING IN PUERTO RICO (AFTER HURRICANE MARÍA)

1.

It's dark now.
September.
Quite cruelly hot.

2.

Barreling down streets full of large chunks
of black tangled wires, shattered glass,
and splintered stop signs,
I swing from lane to lane,
crisscrossing across the double yellow lines
like bursting lattices.
Now that the earth has fallen around me,
my car crushes all that is underfoot.
Locked into its roaring appetite,
the tires take the asphalt prisoner,
shake the concrete barriers,
and gather the flesh of gravel pebbles.

3.

And here in a land without traffic lights
there is a firm shade of understanding,
so that my car chops like a chainsaw,
forging a new path in the sea of debris.
In this season of hurricanes, I grow fearless:
a warrior consuming one road after another.

MY GRANDMOTHER'S PHOTO

She smiles in black and white,
cotton pleated dress with a thick belt,
showing her newlywed 25-inch waist,
a size four, long before the folds
of stretched skin from three children.

Her ebony hair hangs in shiny cascading ringlets,
held by a slip of red ribbon and crystal combs.
Her hand is wrapped tightly around my
grandfather's. New gold branding their
fingers, paid for by the weight of dirt
and hot dawn mornings.

With just one day, the rain washes
out my grandmother's body
and makes her a false whisper upon inspection.
Brown dots replace her smile
and her hands are swallowed
by dark spirals and bubbles.
The thin edges fall into wrinkled tatters,
sprinkles of paper breaking faster
from sheets of water. The wind pushes
her, cracked and rearranged beside an
overturned car like a new broken
flower in the grave.

ANTES/DESPUÉS HURACÁN MARÍA

El Nuevo Día fashioned galaxies
      of before and after photos
           poised for us to study.

      Once I sat in a garden with grass
fanned across my chest.
           I trapped dirt between my toes
    and squeezed   unaware of a time
        where wind   would crush spaces
      standing green.

Blackouts struck zip code   after zip code
      like a willing animal.

      To handwash clothes   in Ace and Suavitel.
        To sprinkle Fabuloso   across the terraza.
      Fruity florals
        to block la planta's foul invasion.

Antes/después conversaciones:
      antes/después edificios
      antes/después tiendas
      antes/después escuelas
      antes/después personas
      antes/después montañas
        antes/después ríos
        antes/después yerba

    Beneath a cielo   where we   the watchers
    learn how to become fluent
      in prayer
        all by ourselves.

THE Q AND A SECTION

If you ask me why I left Puerto Rico,
I would tell you that it wasn't because
Hurricane María left me with a bloated album
of waiting for the black black blackouts
to skip between the trees. It wasn't because
the roofs unfurled and the doors retreated to hollows
somewhere in the sky. It wasn't because
of the shelves of water, inching like new constellations
across an endless night. It was the full circle
of fear, the kind that stays in my mouth
like neon jawbreakers, refusing to surrender, tailor-made
to dislocate words that I long to speak. I dread
colliding against this familiar: when the memory gathers
like burning hands around your throat.

When you tap the muscle memory of the blue tarp

that was supposed to be a temporary roof
but broke, so you moved into the school shelter
but stayed up all night because you were afraid
at how the men looked at you like something on
the clearance rack and then some cousin of a cousin
said that you could come to New York on an
amnesty flight and your other cousin of a cousin
got you on board and you said,

This is it. I'm home. But home turned
into, Where are you from and where are your papers?
I'm an American citizen. I'm Puerto Rican.
This ID looks fake to me. Next.

So, you are told that no one stays here
for free. And then you get a job paying minimum
wage, even though you know that you should be
paid more. And during your fifteen-minute break,
you stare at the lamp posts and pretend that they
are palm trees from your island. A tear falls and
someone says that there's no time to cry. Besides,
tears are not meant for brown girls. You have to
get back to your shift because there are bills to pay
and you want that return ticket, which isn't cheap.

CYCLONE #9

comes on the back / end debris
of 2 am with the creeping rub
wind and a hard / pressed memory
of Hurricane María / inflamed
on a night of empty stars / you
make the rounds to curve the best
part of this story / no lights / no
water / just javelins of wind and
rain / an hourglass of wondering
what will go / windows / doors /
roof / I'm trying to think of the
punchline / something about
hurricanes / nephrologists / and
double whiskey sours / but I think
I'm a prisoner of the what to remember
and what to forget hypothesis / I'm
eyeing an exit / as if to say this
storm will not teach me how to wait

PROMISES

we want hurricane season to shrug //: into a
shut statement //: say won't be a bother
at all //: won't topple trees like fingers without
shame //: crumple houses like new boots looking
for an old trail //: Con calma //: Respira //: we
want hurricane season to give //: better odds of
windowsill waiting //: say won't ransack cupboards
like some errant guest visitor //: won't come
uninvited like noise jumping in children's clothes //: Es
cierto //: Seguro //: we want hurricane season to
evaporate //: like distilled memory vapor //: and
shoestring tie up into history books like velcroed
rough stars //: promise a season without fresh
batteries //: flatfooted //: promise a season without
bloody fingerprints //: soft-boiled //: promise //:

HURRICANE

after Wallace Stevens

Among the leafy hills,
The only moving thing
Was the tentacle of the hurricane.

We are of several oceans,
Like a season
In which there are too many hurricanes.

The hurricane pummeled the trees.
It was an insidious part of the wind.

Water and people
Are circle.
Water and people and hurricanes
Are circle.

We do not know which to pray for first,
The unbruising of earth
Or the unbruising of homes.
The hurricane slumping
Or just after.

Ice cubes disappear in blackouts
With unblemished fruits.
The rubble of the hurricane
Scatters, to and fro.
The warning
Scrolled in the whir
An unquestionable cause.

O frightened Boricuas,
Why do you coordinate maps?
Do you not see how the hurricane
Rapidly strips the steel
Of the bridges beside you?

I know fearless winds
And downed, snapped lights.
But I know, too,
That the hurricane is involved
In what I know.

When the hurricane spread neck-deep water,
It marked the drowning
Of one of many stars.

At the blow of a hurricane
Mounting its claws,
All roofs in Puerto Rico
Leaped away.

We measure our fear
By the windows.
Once, we turned our backs,
In that we presumed
The face of a rainshower
For a hurricane.

The wind is fleeing.
The hurricane must be dimming.

It was spring all September.
It was raining
And it was going to rain.
The hurricane curls
In our ragged throat.

BY EVERYTHING ELSE

DROWNING IN 5 PARTS

We have always been drowning—

With sweat.
With fear.
With debt.

How much for freedom? It's a trick question. You can never pay enough. You will always owe someone or something.

Haiti paid France $30 billion for its independence.

Puerto Rico: How much can I pay?

US: Give me your land, people, language, food, culture, and flag. Maybe then we'll talk.

Puerto Rico: No es justo.

US: Take it or leave it.

Our dreams are free.

We run like stray horses in the mountains. No light for good luck. Who needs it anyway? When there's no want of stars to give us lifeblood.

Sometimes, every so often, a tourist drowns behind a hotel in Condado. The ocean reclaims what it wants. Saying, Here is salt. Take that back in your suitcase. How cruel. How unkind. What does it come to.

•

I was taught to love water. Respect it like your blood. If blood is red, then water is nucleus red. Like ATP red.

All things come from water. All things return to water.

Turn off the faucet. That could be your great-great-grandmother there.

Is it possible to have too much water? Ask the trees. Like during hurricanes.

We should then love and fear water. How can it be both? A kiss and knuckle? Hug and slap? Push and all pull?

You've seen the drowning. Rivers of trees and earth.

Repeat after me. Repeat after me.

Water is my first love.

Me: I ♡ you.

Water: I ♡ you too.

What comes next?

I thought you knew.

•

In the end, only water remained.

But even that was dangerous.

Look at Flint. Look at Standing Rock. Look at Puerto Rico.

What would the ancestors say?

How did we end up here?

They took our land away from us—
repackaged it with manicured lawns,
but kept the pillars and the names plantation and antebellum.
Some gringo names that sound good when you're showing off
to the customer service representative. I live there.
Took our bodies away from us—
rebranded as one flashy R&B star and a basketball player. We
can't all be like that. Even though many of us have dancing
TikTok fantasies and think we're Dr. J's dunking twin. Nope. Just
wounded ankles and knees.

Where are we?

It's June. Water is coming. Let's hope it's not too much. We've been
drowning since forever.

•

What you say about water is what you know.

How can too much water be a bad thing?

Isn't it like love? Having a lot of love is good?

Ask the flowers that go rootless.

Ask the worms that get plucked by birds.

Ask the slaves wa ter wat er waaaa t er.

You don't understand. It's answer D on the test. All of the above.

If hurricanes could speak. Give you the 5-star treatment at the
spa. Tell you the comeback story. Which everyone loves. To forget
the dry run drownings.

•

How you treat water is how you treat your mother.

Treat it kindly, gently.
Don't abuse it.
Don't take it for granted.
It is not going to stay up late and wait for you.
Don't let it run forever.
Even water gets tired and needs a nap.
Sing to it. Be sweet. Tell it how pretty it looks on a nice day.
Bring it flowers just because. Not the $4.99 cheap ones from
Walmart. Something from the garden. So water would say, I
recognize my work. Thank you very much.
Take it to Splash Mountain and watch how people delight
when crashing in chlorinated-with-who-knows-what wetness.
Skip the museum though. There's no need to see children slurp
fountain liquid that is the wrong color. Water would demand
better—How can I look like that? Where is the filter? Shakes head.

Go to church instead. A sprinkle across a baby's bald head.
Time to save souls. Don't ask, and how did the church save
you? To avoid any stink eyes and pops upside the head.
Remember to respect water.

Respect water. Always remember. In the ocean, don't forget
about the undertows. Don't swim too far. The currents.
Teaching you how not to drown. To breathe. Not to drown.
Respect. Respect is a motherfucker.

IN INHERITANCE OF DROWNING

//

They arrived. They arrived on boats. They arrived. Well-lit our Cacique Agüeybaná. Punctuated our Arawak ways. Walloped our waters. Punched down our language. Until our words got washed. Until our tongues got tired. Until our tracheas got thick. Until we forgot that Columbus was a sore winner and loser. Gold for our drowning. We ran after the holler.

//

The owners arrived in fact-checking hats. Demanded we get thrown overboard. Not worth any sorry salt. Like we could refuse this shackled cloakroom. No crawl space to moan. We caught our syllables before the currents black-bottomed. Waaaa terrrr. Wattttt e rrrrrrr. Wa t eeeeer. Let our larynges become rafts. This is the price of drowning.

//

The soldiers arrived in cheap suits. Demanded we leave our land. Abandon our homes. Go many miles. Like our corn had always been in the wrong place. On the trail, we got thirsty. And asked for water. They laughed. *Drink your tears.* We crossed the river. Let our blood become water. We will name our own drowning.

//

How many ways can we drown? You know the answer. No peeking.

DARK MATTER

They don't really care about the Black bodies that go missing,

Victoria Shaw / Teandah Slater / Areall Murchinson / 36.7%
75,000

snipped beyond the wind-dried dandelions. They're not like
the loaded discovery of cool candy-cotton exoplanets.

There's no NASA team to pinpoint their endnote existence on flash bang
satellites. Instead, they are throwaway slick monosyllables,

contorted algorithms, desperate silences that go hungry,
rainwater flecks succumbed to hardwired alleyways,

liquid names cast out in the undertows' peripheries,
the runoff layer of things brimming in the permanent cages of TON 618.

EVERYDAY DROWNING

after Camille Rankine

1.

with open hands
with closed hands
in a church
in a field
as children
as elders
in the front yard
in the backyard
inside of a cell
outside of a cell
in the back of a car
in the front of a car
down an alley
gone joyriding
gone bird watching
gone walking
on the pavement
with screams
with wails
in hashtags
in brokenness
with some limbs
with no limbs
on our feet
off our feet
as parents
motherless
in any city

in our homes
on any day
at anytime
on the news
in blood
without blood
with air
without air
inside the law
outside the law
on a warm day
on a cold day
waiting
at any cardinal direction
with questions
without questions
in quiet
in plain sight
gone from history
in prayer
without prayer
gone slowly
gone quickly

2.

drownings unfold through television
newspapers   video
double-yellow onto roads and sidewalks

bodies cut away
heat of too-close gun
I'm afraid to see and unsee

a future
where blood is kept
inside of the body

a poem beginning and ending
with Black joy
not incomplete
articles of our drownings
as good blue meat

and we can't escape the drownings
determined to handcuff
us below sea level
tell me how
before visiting hours
to mercy fail

perhaps the only way to survive
is to defy water's gravity
count our heartbeats
open eyes to water
reimagine Black bodies
even those that cannot ferry back

3.

Tanisha Anderson
Ahmaud Arbery
Sean Bell
Sandra Bland
Rumain Brisbon
Rayshard Brooks
Andrew Brown Jr.
Cornelius Brown
Michael Brown Jr.
Paterson Brown
Leroy Browning
James Carney III
Philando Castile
Jason Champion
William Chapman
Terry Lee Chatman
Keith Childress

Eddie Clark III
Jamar Clark
Stephon Clark
John Crawford III
Tyree Crawford
Amadou Diallo
Samuel Dubose
Aidan Ellison
Joshua Feast
Jonathan Ferrell
George Floyd
Ezell Ford
Terrance Franklin
Eric Garner
Casey Goodson Jr.
Oscar Grant
Freddie Gray

Ronald Greene
Akai Gurley
Dontre Hamilton
Eric Harris
Kevin Higgenbotham
Andre Hill
Dominic Hutchinson
Kris Jackson
Botham Jean
Atatiana Jefferson
Bettie Jones
Christopher Kimble
Cameron Lamb
Nuwnah LaRoche
Donovan Lewis
Amir Locke
Michael Lee Marshall

Trayvon Martin
Kevin Matthews
David McAtee
Spencer McCain
Willie McCoy
Tony McDade
Laquan McDonald
Keith McLeod
Roy Nelson
Michael Noel
Bryan Overstreet
Dante Parker
Nathaniel H. Pickett II
Jonathan Price
Daniel Prude
Sean Reed
Calvon "Andre" Reid

Jerame Reid
Tamir Rice
Jemel Roberson
Tony Robinson
Troy Robinson
Johnathan Sanders
Walter Scott
Alonzo Smith
Jamal Sutherland
Breonna Taylor
Christian Taylor
Jayland Walker
Walter Wallace Jr.
Patrick Warren
Wayne Wheeler
Phillip White
Daunte Wright
[. . .]

4.

gone quickly
gone slowly
without prayer
in prayer
gone from history
in plain sight
in quiet
without questions
with questions
at any cardinal direction
waiting
on a cold day
on a warm day
outside the law
inside the law
without air
with air
without blood
in blood
on the news
at anytime
on any day
in our homes
in any city
motherless
as parents
off our feet
on our feet
with no limbs
with some limbs
in brokenness
in hashtags

with wails
with screams
on the pavement
gone walking
gone bird watching
gone joyriding
down an alley
in the front of a car
in the back of a car
outside of a cell
inside of a cell
in the backyard
in the front yard
as elders
as children
in a field
in a church
with closed hands
with open hands

A RESPONSE TO WHAT HAPPENS BEFORE WE DROWN

we look in a tight drum a drum
that shivers our windblown Taíno names

winding silently as water cutters
canoe rides that cut ceiba that snap snaps

into folds of three like roll call nagua
skirts shirking lazuline stars that lend to

white stars that white out my larynx out
in Jayuya and Utuado I remember members of

sun Yucahú embers that awakened green
green coquí green capillaries of creek creaking

skybysky it is well known that skybysky
is faultless faults shift our legs on the dashboard

until they dash off bootlegged colorful
drowning who knew death could be an iris

For the Black woman that has laundry lists of tears

and they fill pocketbooks and they run down pantyhose
and they stick to good leather shoes and they occupy Sunday
and they line church pews and they drip onto candles
but you still remember to pray   even though
sickandtiredsickandtiredsosickandtiredverysickand
tiredtoosickandtiredjusttootoosickandtired   and try
to unchoke on the many minuses!$^\infty$ that become
worm food   that come come into come into what
tears that grip the   five pounds of grease on daughters'
scalps runny scratches on auntie's wooden suitcases
ripped exhales on grandmama's stoop   tears un/re/dis/squelched
like B-I-N-G-O   that are certain certainly for certain

COLUMBUS 2020

Down, down, with la Niña, la Pinta, and la Santa María.
Bring the ropes to double snap the memory of what he
said that he discovered. The geometric shapes of his
wingspan lies are hurled into the river, but the lost
native bodies cannot swim ashore. I know that history
books inhale your whiplash of foreign lands and color
the pages with your pockets sucking gold coins. Yes, I
can count how you attached your name to everything
like refrains of the Beatles. Columbus, the great!
Columbus, the bold! Up, up went the sheets of iron
in Buenos Aires, Genova, Salamanca, Richmond,
and Vancouver—just to name a few. But now, the
chains are fitting you again. First, the head falls,
then the hands are spray-painted scarlet, and next
the base rocks. Someone gives it a shove until it
hits the checkpoint of giving way to vertical hands.
They want to take back what is theirs, reclaim all
that fell like beheaded fruit from the bed of the pickup
truck. Into the ocean, into the ocean, down into the
ocean you go, a wrought legacy with a rusted tongue.

PROMESA

after snipped promises
and
birthing lies to
collect debt that
drowns   and
exhausts us   your
flimsy excuses packaged in
green   you—
highest bidders to debone landmarks   you—
in colonial
jackets   a
known presence
loud to rake over our voices   and
mute mercy
protests sprout
quickly
revoke PROMESA
spawls across graffitied walls   calls for you
to take back your triple-pressed boots   on our necks
unsheathing a
vested version   of a territory (really a colony!)
with jeweled oceans   and   crowns of
xenia
you—
year-round master of money
you—
zested with interest
you've never held the rope around so many
zeros before

WHILE BLACK

driving while Black

entering your own house/apartment/business while Black

mourning while Black

listening to music while Black

using a coupon while Black

smoking while Black

flying on an airplane while Black

swimming while Black

canvassing while Black

babysitting while Black

parking while Black

using "free" Wi-Fi while Black

playing while Black

eating while Black

working while Black

walking while Black

golfing while Black

sitting while Black

watching birds while Black

opening a business while Black

cashing a check while Black

reading while Black
talking while Black
laughing while Black
shopping while Black
waiting for a taxi/car service/ride while Black
moving into/buying a new house/apartment/condo while Black
banking while Black
barbecuing while Black
jogging while Black
studying while Black
sleeping while Black
gathering flowers while Black
watering flowers while Black
asking for directions while Black
using a credit card while Black
picking apples while Black
selling loose cigarettes/water/any goods while Black
breathing while Black
existing   while Black

double Black
blackity Black
every shade of Black
Black∞

43

DOCTORS ON TELEVISION RECOMMEND BOOSTER SHOTS BECAUSE THE PANDEMIC IS FAR FROM BEING OVER

Flashpoints of morning rush to take the front seat.
The rapid-fire warnings: bodies belly-up, deaths
without shields, morgues just around the block.

Here's hope getting lost in the statistics. I'd rather hold up
among the loose lies where I pretend I have a better
correspondence with my house. Leave it love notes
by the shower and refrigerator and enjoy compliments
on my ~~pandemic~~ stay-at-home socks. And my children
do not inch through play without hope. Frail wagons
towing kingdoms of damp sand. Collapsed basketballs
surviving savage toss territories. They twirl unbothered
by the virus animal pressing its face against the windows,
waiting to pry our banner of resistance when we sleep.
So we drift onwards in a house that escapes from drowning,
show up on land with news awake in the background.

[1ST] UPON ARRIVAL

Drowning upon arrival is the worst story.

//

Always drowning. C'mon. C'mon. They tongue-tied the oxygen. Move along. We left our homes. Went on the trail. Some escaped to the mountains. They read 3,000, no 4,000, no 5,000. 6,000+ more likely. Died. Tsali will tell them that it was a stampede of death. The river wanted to be fed. So they gave it our skin. It wasn't a wager at all. They said. Sure. Sure. To the river. What were you nursing here? Let it be under water.

//

But no one had to tell us. We just knew. You're dead if you look them in the eyes. You're dead if you leave town and go on the trail. But you're dead anyway, if you stay. They don't even tug at their suits. When they circle back to the rivers of our loss. We don't want your kind here. We don't want your language here. We don't want your ways here. We don't want you here. On Earth. Go to another planet. And hope that we will not land there.

//

Some settled in Oklahoma. Arizona. New Mexico. We left. We left our clay pots, black-on-black. What would María Martínez have told us? They were things meant to be carried. Now, they had a good view of the soldiers' boots. We left before the river claimed more bodies. No bodies, no cry. We left before the river became a secret book with deadbolt bones. We left. That when said. We would not disturb the river. Even if they gave it back to us.

BECOMING AMERICAN

We are first to cover our hearts
with our hands, sing "My Country,
'Tis of Thee," and wear la Americana flag shorts.

We swap Medalla for Budweiser. Go to Shoney's
and order the all-you-can eat breakfast. No one
cares if we waste food as long as we leave a decent
tip and speak quietly. Leave La Isla's conversaciones
at the kitchen table. We are encouraged to buy the biggest
trucks and waste gas. Take over the road and parking
spaces. People make way when they see us. What kind
of horsepower do you get? They admire strength.

We are told not to ask those back home to send us
pique and café. We should tamper our tongues
and get the mild options. We go to Starbucks
and get wild concoctions like unicorn berry frappuccino.
Everything tastes too sweet. But this, they say,
is the American way. Sugar. Sugar. More sugar.

Our coworkers just go ahead and call us JL
and AE because they butcher our real names
Josefa Luz and Agapito Efraín. Everyone goes by some
initials anyway, they claim. Look at JFK and MLK.
Juanito is Buddy. Everyone here gets a nickname too.

We are forgetting the cuentos about the iguana thief.
Now, it's blah, blah, blah about parking as wide
as bedrooms. Rows and rows of different types
of water in stores. Community meetings with five
different types of cake and strawberry swirl ice cream.
Everything is so sweet, but they give us plates
swathed in foil. It is the American way.

Some signs say English only, no Spanish allowed.
There is the look to keep our rolling *rrrrr*s to ourselves.
Pronounce rice so that it doesn't sound like fries.
Remember it's soup or salad (not super salad).
And delete the word focus from our vocabulary
(it always sounds like fuck us). The waiter smiles
when we leave a nice tip. Because tipping is the American
way. Please come again. Take some mints. Here are the toothpicks.
Goodies on the way out. How nice. How American.

The junk mail is bigger and brighter. The flyer
from the neighborhood dentist pops orange in chili pepper
font with promises to make teeth white, white, white!
The flyer comes with a coupon, a special, something
on sale. How can it be any more American than that?

RETURN

The river said, I'll protect you and give you shelter. So we migrants came.

•

We traveled a long journey. The river carried us like familiar wind. Then we walked and dreamed of motionless water. Dreamed of water that said welcome. Come. Come. Come.

•

Then they arrived with hanging scowls. Arrived on horses long-reined with whips. Ran down our Black bodies. Trampled our faces. Maimed our voices. Made us turn our backs to water. Told us, Water will not protect you here. This water does not belong to you. Your tears belong to you. That water is yours. That water should be plenty.

•

Our tears scramble across miles. They get caught in many rivers. And our bodies. Our bodies keep drowning. We die in so many ways.

•

They say we have no papers, no roots to dayfall here, as we are being sent back.

•

We see the water below us on the plane. It tells us to return. Think of tendrils pushing through the muddy bottom. We can't look away.

WHERE LOSS BEGINS AT THE BORDER

A failure of stars
wreck of moon
too dim to see land
drowning erases our reflections

hurt ghosts wear the same clothing
animals to be interrupted

shelters unable to shake out a prayer
hope folded down with a foil blanket

corpses crust atop salt water
yolas collapse onto bleached sand

death leaves a film so faint
that it might as well
dissolve into a bird's mouth

a damp echo

               loss begins at the border

           failure of stars
         wreck of moon
         too dim
         drowning erases   reflections

                    wear the same clothing
        animals   interrupted

                  shake out a prayer
            folded down

        corpses crust
        yolas collapse

death   so faint
        might
dissolve   bird's mouth

    damp echo
                    at the border

            failure
            wreck
            too dim
            drowning erases

                    clothing

                            prayer

            corpses
            yolas

            death

            dissolve

                    echo

                            border

                        dim
                        drowning

            death

                    echo

ARCHIVE OF GREEN

I'm afraid to squint
the green morning.
Kingfishers spill
into trees. Grass churns
their interrupted wings.
My vomit gropes green–
conceived gallstones.
Doctors growl *no green money,*
no service. Officers grunt
no green card, no mercy.
Deportation agents hiss
sit in the green chair.
Their eyes upend jaded faces
to riot. How green precedes
guideposts to exile.

LA PELUQUERÍA

On my seventh birthday,
my tía took me to the

beauty salon to get an
alisado. It's time that you

got rid of that pelo malo,
she winked like a full

moon stretching above the
sky. Her friend Puchi stirred

a white creamy concoction
and smeared it over my

scalp like flowering foreign
watercolors. How long must

it stay on? Just until it binds
the curl. But what I heard

was, until oppression flattens
me like cardboard constellations

and makes me burn my
history like inkblots of

pretzeled fists. Just think
of what you are going to

look like. In their minds, I
am wearing a headdress

of glass layers that stays in
place and refuses to rise

in humidity. In their world,
my hair is no longer a Greek

tragedy or bad penny tossed
into the gutter. It is a parable

of dignity, an escape route from
being just another brown girl.

STREET MEDITATION

In my rust-ringed Mitsubishi Mirage, a gift from a cousin's
cousin who never saw any promise of seventeen from the lineup
of trauma:

- ☑ dengue
- ☑ zika
- ☑ chikungunya
- ☐ diabetes
- ☑ hurricanes
- ☑ earthquakes
- ☐ COVID-19

Not alcohol or drugs like run-of the-mill folks. Sometimes, I
don't want to write about it. I would rather spy on my favorite
pothole grooves on la Avenida De Diego and the trees that got
lured there. 'Cause even the street wants green love. When I go
cruising, I look for bodies that overgrow their wounds—those
swathed in gold chains with a sparkle not needing to be rescued.
What's happening tonight: Daddy Yankee, Tego, Don Omar, Ivy
Queen, and Wisin & Yandel punctuating the reguetón reunion
tour—the fastest sequence to fun:

- ☑ tickets in the ~~front row~~ nosebleed section
- ☑ selfie poses with cardboard cutouts
- ☐ backstage access
- ☑ autographs (preprinted in the concert program!)
- ☑ perreo
- ☐ tattoos
- ☐ new piercings
- ☑ Don Q at La Factoría

My runaway tongue matches the dembow. A green light to
drown in sweat. Blot out all enemies and offer them up in smoke.

GHOST TALKER POEM

And for the Black girls
that go missing from
newspaper headlines and
spotlight 5 pm news. What
happened to them? Kick
the can over. See if the bones
glint in the slips of sunshine.
Press your ears against the
grass. Listen to what bleeds.

My mother in her lovely
tongue. Those girls are
probably with friends. Hanging
out in the basement. Wearing
cigarette pants. Cigarette
pants were fashionable once.

They will turn up. Like loose
change sidelined under sofa
cushions. Overdue books
sandwiched in sweaters. Favorite
hairpins gagged by vents.

Don't fret. Fret is a funny word
for a young child. Sounds like
forget. Don't forget. I won't.
About the missing Black girls.
Probably already dead. In a
ditch. Or a field somewhere.

I'm not supposed to think about
death. Passing away. Kicked
the bucket. 6 feet under. Meeting

our maker. Which is what my
teacher said. The class guinea pig
had stopped moving. Mrs. Hayes
poked its feet. And then shoved it
into a shoebox. Said that we could
bury it across from the tire swing. In
the back of the school yard. The
dirt was ordinary. Brown. Hard.

Eat your snack, said my mother.
Twinkies. From 7-Eleven. Maybe
Wawa. Nothing from SuperFresh
or Pathmark. White filling. Creamy
like white fungus. Oozing like
zit puss. Besmirching golden cake.

The news says nothing about
Black girls that go missing. Not
even a speck in someone's
unread newspaper. Silence is
when we inherit ghosts. I see them
taking victory laps every night.

MAD LOVE FOR PHILLY

some beg for money on the concrete
by Locust Street, but I would become wingless
for a layered hoagie with extra pickles
and a pretzel from some hazy vendor
never mind, blood on sidewalk
spills like a flogged star

//

the boot came for John Wanamaker,
Gimbels, and Strawbridge & Clothier
but I don't mind   the old Gallery is still the place to be
the best light for homeless to stay warm and daydream

//

street-level with imperfect door grilles

corner stores with Now and Laters and Tastykakes and
Italian water Icees and Mister Softee trucks and
Peking duck in Chinatown windows and
hippy-dippy vintage shops on South Street
spaces that stall shootings and arcs of violence

//

boom   I'm cannonballing away from
abandoned rowhouses into Fairmount Park
and Penn Relay and the Betsy Ross House
like a fresh philosophy attracting crowds
no forecasts of police and red repeat concrete today

//

I pass the sirens on Wadsworth Avenue
and Broad and Olney to men playing hoops
with bald rims and then no rims

//

1-2-3   bob double dutch feet and
glisten laughter   dirty pigeons gridlock
the graffitied LOVE statue

//

I'm in the 76ers' house surefiring Embiid and
then Germantown trolleying across protests
to the 105.3 FM Quiet Storm
like a gesture carrying no apologies

//

Philly, you're my ride or die thing
love begets love thing   except when
Black people get bombed and Black people get shot
and Black men at Starbucks get arrested
for just minding their own damn business

//

Philly, I give you a poem
with Black-skinned meaning
a home I freed for the selves
when they are closest to touch

DECUSSATE

I'm not saying violence isn't wrong, but I understand it.

Mrs. Hayes is quick to remind us:
We should never put our hands on anyone.
Violence is never the answer.
Then she loads the projector.
The film crackles on the screen.
Of muskets and cannons—
instruments from a war where
the thirteen colonies gained their freedom
by killing men in red—
red like bright breasts of birds
red like big-boned leaves on trees.

Why couldn't they ask King George
for their independence?
Carol wants to know.
Didn't they ask nicely?

The film sputter-turns to the Civil War
and bombards us with red over blue
and gray garments. Men getting pummeled
and slaves hoping for a quiltwork of freedom.
Slaves that never had a prelude of asking nicely.
Slaves that swept the dust in breath,
while masters kneed them dreamless.

Mrs. Hayes has her hands on her hips.
Like my own mother.
When the guidance counselor told her
that I would never get accepted by an Ivy League college.
Her eyes stripping Mr. Connor to a bare letter.
His hands on my mother's shoulders
and the firm brushing away of fat fingers.

The woman's patience chafed her legs, but not her voice.
After two hours of waiting for the doctor,
she screamed and pounded her fists at the counter.
The doctor will see you now, the receptionist's eyes
widened into black moons.
Then a buzz to let her through.
The rest of us clutching our shell-shocked papers.

The group of men circled the heart-shaped train rider,
until she spit-shined a knife and caught a rib.
The men dodged like rodeo clowns.

I think of my mother.
The neighbors when they were told
their children threw stones and dirt into our pool.
My mother's tongue slicing them in a stroke ending.
Her tongue taking the place of fists.
Tell us when to send the cleanup crew, they said.

I understand violence.
It starts as the introduction to many wounds.
You could press down hard enough, if one bleeds:
Aiyana
Atatiana
Breonna
Fred
Malcolm
Martin
Medgar
Sandra
Trayvon
Yvette

They killed our best people.

Until the mouths no longer hold stones,
when the hands are pure,
red will be a color
as good
with good
across good.

SHAME IN THE SHADE OF BLUE

1.

There are Black bodies playing in the sunlight,
when the sirens come. They cut us like roots
from crushed trees, chop us into what is left of
the sky—how our wounds gather
                            into hashtags
                                    protests
                                    prayers
                                            tall waiting
                                                    of justice
                                                    equality
                                                    respect
                            on earth.

2.

This is the same story.

There are Black bodies leaping across the grass,
when the men in dark blue shatter the seconds,
handcuffing everything in sight. The punches
come pouring, then knees and feet arrive to the
heads, until the bodies spin and fall back to
snap the cruisers' windshields.

3.

Listen, whatever you do, stay calm.

These are the instructions you have been
told all of your life, but the fear still surges
through you as your breath sprints away. You
are like a child again, peeing your pants.

4.

I can't imagine that you believe their
doo-wop of reasons. When you split
beneath the surface, you will know
what I mean.

LIVING IN PUERTO RICO IS AS CLOSE AS I CAN GET TO LIVING IN THE UNITED STATES

I tell you this while letting the butter brown

and pouring the pancake batter on the too-ready griddle.

This is no joking matter.

What is there for me?

Don't you miss the trip to Skyline Drive in September?

The time to see the too-bright yellows, burnt purples, and almost-gaudy oranges?

Temporary beauty cannot lure me.

It's a daytrap.

•

Years ago, I settled for fall. I lived in a quiet town, on a quiet street, in a quiet house.

The leaves shook everything awake. Made me think of earth's muscle.

How it flashed different colors. I gave it a high-five. Said, come here, new love.

Please talk about yourself. Fall stayed until winter moved in and shared a sink. It was bossy.

Demanded that I put salt on the sidewalks, so that no one would slip.

•

I understand quiet. I know how to recognize quiet in many places.

It wears old house dresses and then comes to church on Sunday for
doughnuts

and blueberry bottom cake. Sometimes, we could be identical twins.

But I prefer sugar cookie cake with hot pink frosting. I do not tell quiet

because quiet would frown. Quiet would tell me to not make a
fuss. Be out of sight.

Is that the same as invisible? Quiet stays quiet.

•

Quiet is when I lived in a quiet town, on a quiet street, in a quiet house

until I forgot how to speak. I couldn't say my name when the police
asked me

what I was doing in the house. Was I the maid? Oh, you live here?

The incredulity unreeling in the voice was not quiet at all. Neither
were my tears.

Please don't shoot me.

Please don't kill me in this quiet town, on a quiet street, in a quiet house.

•

In Puerto Rico, my house dresses are too-loud red.

I scream, "Ay, Ay, Ay!" when the neighbor tells me chisme.

And when September comes, I don't let the hurricanes holler alone.

CLEANLINESS

On the flight to San Juan, the tourists sitting next to me remark how good I smell. It's the same perfume Rihanna wears. *Oh. You know some celebrities don't believe in that. They don't sprinkle any Jean Naté or bathe. They don't bathe their children either.*

I wasn't raised like that. The first thing my parents did, after paying all the bills and getting my school supplies, was making sure that I had three washcloths to my name: one for the face, one for the body, and one for the feet. Cleanliness next to godliness was always in the first person. So, I was clean. The house was clean. My name was clean.

At my first job, the boss leaned in closely to smell the Ivory soap on my skin. I don't think he had seen someone like me in the office before. How clean was the response! My coworkers checked for dirt under my nails when I ate lunch. I don't think they had seen someone like me in the office before. How clean was the response!

How clean was the pass key to a good job, good house, good future. We couldn't afford to be associated with dirt. The rumor was enough to set us back—be

a) arrested
b) kicked out
c) spat at
d) beaten up
e) all of the above

Never thought I would see celebrities bragging about being dirty. Only the rich would do that!

The rest of us horde miniature soaps and bottled water. When they ask us about cleanliness, we show them the rows of toiletries.

SPENT

To stand in line on a Tuesday,
while the moon at the coda
of the 4 am edge glistens saffron,
and wait for the food bank
to open at 7 am is no easy burden.
I breathe in my reality
and place it in my mouth:
the remaining can of tomato sauce
and loaf of white bread
cannot fuse my tightening belly,
and I don't have ten dollars to
buy eggs, milk, cereal, and juice.

I stalk the meat at $7 for a pack.
The manager winks, "Still in stock."
My mind pins the clippings of farmers
dumping milk and pushing vegetables
back into the earth. What it must feel like
to stroke the aperture of new cells and then
pivot to carrying skeletons plump
with yearning. Yes, what I see is a strange
arrangement that has hauled itself
into existence on steady prongs,
in the throes of bottomless theories
of the world and dangles on our ears.

TOKEN

I think that I'm your one Black
friend // the one that you corral
into your book clubs or
weekday lunches

like a gesture of shrugged
shoulders // so that you can cut
across the crinoline layers
to crank // see I'm not a

racist because I'm friends with
x // the one that you chisel
with questions //
why do Black people do

this? // why do Black
people think that? // have
you really experienced
racism? // as if I could

jumpstart a new season // where
I'm an expert or // a professor
giving a lecture //
the one you flirt with the

n word // nope // that is not
happening // my face turns
a corner // you look
blunted // like you cannot

understand how this word
huddles // infuses with tragedies
// and rings in my
ears like pregnant choking //

the one that you line up at your
barbecue // so that you have a
warm history posted online //
but it's not necessary

to invite me to your holiday
parties or boat trips // we
disentangle as friends // in
the palest quiet of the word

HOW I LOST MY NAME

Your name Dorsía booms heavy like

wide-eyed darkness / said my teacher /

as if light sat on his tongue / so I

became a ticker tape of nothing to be

called / and vanished into famined

sounds / my classmates / backboned

this death sentence / and left no disguise

of this in // visible girl at an elbow

distance / who waited her turn / like

being asked to slow dance / against

a backdrop of double-edged drowning

BY HURRICANE
REVISITED

REM: A CASE STUDY

The drowning happens now as
wind strong-arms trees. Birds
are witnesses. They screech, don't
leave a red mess. Mercy made a
cameo once. She said time is money
and punch-clocked out. The sky
widens enough to scaffold my
holler. Rain is snuffing out my
stray breath. I see the uncombed
gardens last where only hurricanes stay.

POEM WRITTEN UPON RETURNING TO MY HOME
AFTER A HURRICANE

a waste of green
complex molecules release ugly algorithms
against splattered walls
my eyes bathe in green carnage
buried books
buried clothes
buried furniture
an infestation of merciless dots
choking even the brown out of wood
all it would take is Clorox trained
to debunk hurt and tie up loss
I'm afraid to scrub deeper
for there are more angry green stories
birthing behind every door
reader tell me the shortcut to
a season without green grief   away from
a September lurking
with hard deposits
of what used to be

They came for us

out of the woodwork with their sun-bleached
smiles and sea-sprayed tans, tendons of cash
to trademark residences fatbacking the coast.
In return, bowlegged access to beaches, aerosol
sight of skies, coupon books of what was ours.

on Saturday and Sunday morning commercials
showing jovial kids eating mac n' cheese with
orange sauce and Zucaritas to cut off a foot or
leg later maybe even (sorry, folks!) an eye or
two. Abuela's meals shooed into the other room.

at the invitation of the government. Come to
paradise. And so, they came. And so, they
stayed. And so, they ~~said thanks~~ demanded. And
so, they [destroyed and] conquered. ¿Y qué nos
pasó? Estamos muriendo. Deja de matarnos.

let's have this conversation in English. Those
apparitions are of your own making. If you turn
into a myth, then that's your problem. Look. You
still have the chupacabra. It will not rat you out.
There's your glow-up limb. Now, grow yourself back.

MEMORIES OF CANE

1.

The fields shed blood,
long ribbons matted
with skin and dirt. Your ratoons
burn with shredded placenta
and sunstruck hands. Scar-licks
on your body wait
for the soft tissue to cross over.

2.

Tree trunk veins spiral,
as we collect our machetes.
Hands mask the next bundle,
fast to avoid the pinpricked corners
and jagged stalks. Sweat
commands the air. Our wombs
long to shake awake,
orphan juice in the dirt.

3.

During afternoon tea,
I am asked if I want one lump
or two. Piles of sugar cubes
arranged neatly on white linen
as if to say no blood passed
for us. Sweet hallucinations,
see how we sparkle with your fall.

HURRICANE MARÍA COUNTDOWN

10

The neighbors have gone hunting
for sheets of wood at Home Depot
and water at Walmart.

9

We tape plastic over the windows
and then snap the silver tormenteras
into place: clang, bang, clang.

8

Las noticias on the television recites
the warning: María is coming.
But it wasn't supposed to be this
bad: a whirlwind Category 5.

7

The beach is getting half-eaten.
The seashells drowning in new graves.

6

I do not see a single bird. I grieve.

5

The neighborhood school's windows
and roof get swallowed by a rushing
torrent.

4

Some satos make their way through
the liquid bombs and dash under a
car.

3

Emergency lights flood the airport.
They engulf whatever good humor
was left.

2

Billboards by Plaza Las Américas
rock back and forth like line laundry
before hitting the ground.

1

There is something grinding outside
with a loud rasp. I can barely hear las
noticias' wail about María.

0

The last stench before the power
crawls away.

WIDOWS

Hurricane María made us all widows
but we didn't have to wear black
we were already in mourning
cells bathed in fight or flight
having lost everything to bits
in battlefields of wind-rain clapping
then FEMA arrived with a
boxed lunch and an IOU
for a prepaid cell phone and debit card
forms to fill out asking
for proof of home ownership,
bank account, and identification
before they would even consider our claims
the governor came with
a caravan of camera crews and
wanted to hear our stories not the ones
about huddling in a hot shelter
with expired rice to eat
but the ones about Puerto Rico
being the jewel of the Caribbean
the ones about our towns being
open for business
for what can we widows do
Hurricane María smashed our
prefrontal cortices to whistles of dead air
it is mentioned that we are props flung
against a landmarked plot
the newspapers said that we cried
they didn't say that we woke up drowning

NOTES

In "First Poem Before Hurricanes," the pronunciation and definition of hurricane come from the *Merriam-Webster Dictionary*. The notation about hurricanes also comes from the *Merriam-Webster Dictionary*.

The phrase "Not even a turn to God to rebuke the hours" in "The Awakening of Hurricane María" is influenced by the line in the poem "I'm Not Faking My Astonishment, Honest" by Paige Lewis: "The future refuses to happen, so where else should I turn?"

Haiti paid 150 million francs for its freedom from France. Scholars estimate that this amount would be equivalent to $20-30 billion today.

In "Drowning in 5 Parts," the line "Ask the slaves wa ter wat er waaaa t er" is a reference to M. NourbeSe Philip's *Zong!*

In "In Inheritance of Drowning," the lines "Waaaa terrrr. Wattttt e rrrrrrr. Wa t eeeeer" is a reference to M. NourbeSe Philip's *Zong!*

According to Stacy M. Brown's article, "Our Black Women and Girls Have Gone Missing but Few Seem to Care," Victoria Shaw, Teandah Slater, and Areall Murchinson were among the 242,295 people of color missing in the US in 2016, 36.7% of whom were Black teens under the age 18.

The names in "Everyday Drowning" represent some of the Black people that lost their lives to violent interactions with police and citizens.

PROMESA stands for the Puerto Rico Oversight, Management, and Economic Stability Act. It established a board to oversee how Puerto Rico would restructure its debt, which enacted great measures of austerity.

The phrase "where I pretend I have a better correspondence with my house" in "Doctors on Television Recommend Booster Shots Because the Pandemic Is Far from Being Over" is influenced by a line in the poem "Wonder," by Mei-mei Berssenbrugge: "So, by wonder, they strengthen correspondence between sky and home."

"In Loss Begins at the Border," yolas are small boats.

In "Mad Love for Philly," the line "Black people get bombed" refers to the MOVE bombing, in which six adults and five children were killed in Philadelphia on May 13, 1985. The bombing was ordered by the local police. "Black people get shot" refers to the Black victims of police brutality in Philadelphia, such as William H. Green, Charles Fletcher Janerette Jr., Charles Matthews, Donta Dawson, Ronald Timbers, Abebe Isaac, Jamil Moses, Philippe Holland, and Walter Wallace Jr. "Black men at Starbucks get arrested" refers to the arrest of Rashon Nelson and Donte Robinson at a Philadelphia Starbucks on April 12, 2018.

ACKNOWLEDGMENTS

I am full of deep gratitude to the team at CavanKerry—Joan, Gabe, Dana, Dimitri, and Tamara for their insights, suggestions, and encouragement. What a privilege to share this experience with you. Thank you for being with me at every moment and helping me create something so beautiful. Thank you also to the readers at CavanKerry for first recognizing the significance of this book.

Thank you to Baron Wormser for seeing the wonderful possibilities of this book. I appreciate your generous feedback.

Thank you to Jennifer Lee and Joy Arbor for their keen attention to the many details of this book.

Thank you to Shara McCallum, Frances Richey, and Derrick Austin for your unwavering support and for helping the book shine.

Many thanks to Velma Pollard for your friendship, candor, and advice. It is a blessing that I can always count on you.

Mil gracias to Vincent Toro for his golden words and encouragement. I am unbelievably grateful that the book opens with your brilliance.

Thank you to my instructors, friends, and peers at Bread Loaf, Tin House, Kenyon, Poets and Scholars Summer Writing Retreat, Obsidian Foundation Workshop, and Hudson Valley Writers Center, where some of these poems first started taking shape and others were enhanced.

A million thanks to my family, especially my mother, for cheering me on and being my biggest fans.

Mil gracias to Tony and Antonio—my two hearts—for giving me the space and courage to dream and many hugs along the way.

Thank you, dear reader, for believing in poetry.

And thank you, angels—especially my father.

Many thanks to these publications and staff for their kind support of my poetry and giving my poems the opportunity to shine in their original forms and titles:

Ají Magazine: "What the Poet is Supposed to Write about a Hurricane"
ANMLY: "Drowning in 5 Parts"
The Blue Lake Review: "When you tap the muscle memory of the blue tarp"
Claw & Blossom: "The Bee" and "The Q and A Section"
Cream City Review: "Antes/Después Huracán María," "In Inheritance of Drowning," "A Response to What Happens before We Drown," and "Where Loss Begins at the Border"
Denver Quarterly: "Archive of Green" and "Hurricane"
Fourteen Hills: "Decussate"
Havik: "Litany"
Heartwood Literary Magazine: "Driving in Puerto Rico After Hurricane María"
The Hopper: "Cyclone #9" and "Promises"
Kweli Journal: "First Poem Before Hurricanes"
The minnesota review: "They came for us"
Misfit Magazine: "Token"
Moko: "While Black"
The North Dakota Quarterly: "REM: A Case Study"
Porter House Review: "La Peluquería"
Portland Review: "In Search of Space (After Hurricane María)"
POUI: The Cave Hill Literary Annual: "Memories of Cane" and "My Grandmother's Photo"

The Shore: "Dark Matter"
The Sierra Nevada Review: "For the Black woman that has laundry
    lists of tears"
The Superstition Review: "Columbus 2020"
Terrain: "[1st] Upon Arrival"
Wasafiri: "Ghost Talker Poem"

"The Awakening of Hurricane María" appeared in *Feminist Responses to the Neoliberalization of the University: From Surviving to Thriving* published by Lexington Books.

"Shame in the Shade of Blue" is a part of the Ducktown Poetry Trail with the Noyes Museum of Art of Stockton University.

"Spent" appeared in *In Isolation: An Anthology,* published by Alternative Field and Avenue 50 Studio.

CAVANKERRY'S MISSION

A not-for-profit literary press serving art and community, CavanKerry is committed to expanding the reach of poetry and other fine literature to a general readership by publishing works that explore the emotional and psychological landscapes of everyday life, and to bringing that art to the underserved where they live, work, and receive services.

OTHER BOOKS IN THE EMERGING VOICES SERIES

In Inheritance of Drowning was typeset in Bembo Std, which was created in 1495 by Venetian printer Francesco Griffo. Its modern equivalent was revived in 1929 by historian and designer Stanley Morison.